THiS PLANNER BELONGS TO:

2024

Whenever I think of the past, it brings back so many memories. ~ STEVEN WRIGHT

January 2024
Su	M	Tu	W	Th	F	Sa
	1	2	3	4	5	6
7	8	9	10	11	12	13
14	15	16	17	18	19	20
21	22	23	24	25	26	27
28	29	30	31			

February 2024
Su	M	Tu	W	Th	F	Sa
				1	2	3
4	5	6	7	8	9	10
11	12	13	14	15	16	17
18	19	20	21	22	23	24
25	26	27	28	29		

March 2024
Su	M	Tu	W	Th	F	Sa
					1	2
3	4	5	6	7	8	9
10	11	12	13	14	15	16
17	18	19	20	21	22	23
24	25	26	27	28	29	30
31						

April 2024
Su	M	Tu	W	Th	F	Sa
	1	2	3	4	5	6
7	8	9	10	11	12	13
14	15	16	17	18	19	20
21	22	23	24	25	26	27
28	29	30				

May 2024
Su	M	Tu	W	Th	F	Sa
			1	2	3	4
5	6	7	8	9	10	11
12	13	14	15	16	17	18
19	20	21	22	23	24	25
26	27	28	29	30	31	

June 2024
Su	M	Tu	W	Th	F	Sa
						1
2	3	4	5	6	7	8
9	10	11	12	13	14	15
16	17	18	19	20	21	22
23	24	25	26	27	28	29
30						

July 2024
Su	M	Tu	W	Th	F	Sa
	1	2	3	4	5	6
7	8	9	10	11	12	13
14	15	16	17	18	19	20
21	22	23	24	25	26	27
28	29	30	31			

August 2024
Su	M	Tu	W	Th	F	Sa
				1	2	3
4	5	6	7	8	9	10
11	12	13	14	15	16	17
18	19	20	21	22	23	24
25	26	27	28	29	30	31

September 2024
Su	M	Tu	W	Th	F	Sa
1	2	3	4	5	6	7
8	9	10	11	12	13	14
15	16	17	18	19	20	21
22	23	24	25	26	27	28
29	30					

October 2024
Su	M	Tu	W	Th	F	Sa
		1	2	3	4	5
6	7	8	9	10	11	12
13	14	15	16	17	18	19
20	21	22	23	24	25	26
27	28	29	30	31		

November 2024
Su	M	Tu	W	Th	F	Sa
					1	2
3	4	5	6	7	8	9
10	11	12	13	14	15	16
17	18	19	20	21	22	23
24	25	26	27	28	29	30

December 2024
Su	M	Tu	W	Th	F	Sa
1	2	3	4	5	6	7
8	9	10	11	12	13	14
15	16	17	18	19	20	21
22	23	24	25	26	27	28
29	30	31				

2026

Don't. Stop. Thinking about tomorrow. ~ CHRISTINE MCVIE

January 2026
Su	M	Tu	W	Th	F	Sa
				1	2	3
4	5	6	7	8	9	10
11	12	13	14	15	16	17
18	19	20	21	22	23	24
25	26	27	28	29	30	31

February 2026
Su	M	Tu	W	Th	F	Sa
1	2	3	4	5	6	7
8	9	10	11	12	13	14
15	16	17	18	19	20	21
22	23	24	25	26	27	28

March 2026
Su	M	Tu	W	Th	F	Sa
1	2	3	4	5	6	7
8	9	10	11	12	13	14
15	16	17	18	19	20	21
22	23	24	25	26	27	28
29	30	31				

April 2026
Su	M	Tu	W	Th	F	Sa
			1	2	3	4
5	6	7	8	9	10	11
12	13	14	15	16	17	18
19	20	21	22	23	24	25
26	27	28	29	30		

May 2026
Su	M	Tu	W	Th	F	Sa
					1	2
3	4	5	6	7	8	9
10	11	12	13	14	15	16
17	18	19	20	21	22	23
24	25	26	27	28	29	30
31						

June 2026
Su	M	Tu	W	Th	F	Sa
	1	2	3	4	5	6
7	8	9	10	11	12	13
14	15	16	17	18	19	20
21	22	23	24	25	26	27
28	29	30				

July 2026
Su	M	Tu	W	Th	F	Sa
			1	2	3	4
5	6	7	8	9	10	11
12	13	14	15	16	17	18
19	20	21	22	23	24	25
26	27	28	29	30	31	

August 2026
Su	M	Tu	W	Th	F	Sa
						1
2	3	4	5	6	7	8
9	10	11	12	13	14	15
16	17	18	19	20	21	22
23	24	25	26	27	28	29
30	31					

September 2026
Su	M	Tu	W	Th	F	Sa
		1	2	3	4	5
6	7	8	9	10	11	12
13	14	15	16	17	18	19
20	21	22	23	24	25	26
27	28	29	30			

October 2026
Su	M	Tu	W	Th	F	Sa
				1	2	3
4	5	6	7	8	9	10
11	12	13	14	15	16	17
18	19	20	21	22	23	24
25	26	27	28	29	30	31

November 2026
Su	M	Tu	W	Th	F	Sa
1	2	3	4	5	6	7
8	9	10	11	12	13	14
15	16	17	18	19	20	21
22	23	24	25	26	27	28
29	30					

December 2026
Su	M	Tu	W	Th	F	Sa
		1	2	3	4	5
6	7	8	9	10	11	12
13	14	15	16	17	18	19
20	21	22	23	24	25	26
27	28	29	30	31		

~ 2025 ~

January 2025

Su	M	Tu	W	Th	F	Sa
			1	2	3	4
5	6	7	8	9	10	11
12	13	14	15	16	17	18
19	20	21	22	23	24	25
26	27	28	29	30	31	

February 2025

Su	M	Tu	W	Th	F	Sa
						1
2	3	4	5	6	7	8
9	10	11	12	13	14	15
16	17	18	19	20	21	22
23	24	25	26	27	28	

March 2025

Su	M	Tu	W	Th	F	Sa
						1
2	3	4	5	6	7	8
9	10	11	12	13	14	15
16	17	18	19	20	21	22
23	24	25	26	27	28	29
30	31					

April 2025

Su	M	Tu	W	Th	F	Sa
		1	2	3	4	5
6	7	8	9	10	11	12
13	14	15	16	17	18	19
20	21	22	23	24	25	26
27	28	29	30			

May 2025

Su	M	Tu	W	Th	F	Sa
				1	2	3
4	5	6	7	8	9	10
11	12	13	14	15	16	17
18	19	20	21	22	23	24
25	26	27	28	29	30	31

June 2025

Su	M	Tu	W	Th	F	Sa
1	2	3	4	5	6	7
8	9	10	11	12	13	14
15	16	17	18	19	20	21
22	23	24	25	26	27	28
29	30					

July 2025

Su	M	Tu	W	Th	F	Sa
		1	2	3	4	5
6	7	8	9	10	11	12
13	14	15	16	17	18	19
20	21	22	23	24	25	26
27	28	29	30	31		

August 2025

Su	M	Tu	W	Th	F	Sa
					1	2
3	4	5	6	7	8	9
10	11	12	13	14	15	16
17	18	19	20	21	22	23
24	25	26	27	28	29	30
31						

September 2025

Su	M	Tu	W	Th	F	Sa
	1	2	3	4	5	6
7	8	9	10	11	12	13
14	15	16	17	18	19	20
21	22	23	24	25	26	27
28	29	30				

October 2025

Su	M	Tu	W	Th	F	Sa
			1	2	3	4
5	6	7	8	9	10	11
12	13	14	15	16	17	18
19	20	21	22	23	24	25
26	27	28	29	30	31	

November 2025

Su	M	Tu	W	Th	F	Sa
						1
2	3	4	5	6	7	8
9	10	11	12	13	14	15
16	17	18	19	20	21	22
23	24	25	26	27	28	29
30						

December 2025

Su	M	Tu	W	Th	F	Sa
	1	2	3	4	5	6
7	8	9	10	11	12	13
14	15	16	17	18	19	20
21	22	23	24	25	26	27
28	29	30	31			

You have brains in your head. You have feet in your shoes. You can steer yourself any direction you choose. ~ DR. SEUSS

January 2025

December 2024

Su	M	Tu	W	Th	F	Sa
1	2	3	4	5	6	7
8	9	10	11	12	13	14
15	16	17	18	19	20	21
22	23	24	25	26	27	28
29	30	31				

February 2025

Su	M	Tu	W	Th	F	Sa
						1
2	3	4	5	6	7	8
9	10	11	12	13	14	15
16	17	18	19	20	21	22
23	24	25	26	27	28	

Sunday	Monday	Tuesday	Wednesday
IMPORTANT:			
			1 NEW YEAR'S DAY
5 NATIONAL WHIPPED CREAM DAY	**6** NATIONAL CUDDLE UP DAY EPIPHANY	**7** NATIONAL BOBBLEHEAD DAY	**8** HAPPY BIRTHDAY TO ELVIS!
12 NATIONAL KISS A GINGER DAY	**13** NATIONAL RUBBER DUCKY DAY	**14** NATIONAL DRESS UP YOUR PET DAY	**15** NATIONAL HAT DAY
19 NATIONAL POPCORN DAY	**20** NATIONAL DISC JOCKEY DAY MARTIN LUTHER KING JR DAY	**21** SQUIRREL APPRECIATION DAY	**22** NATIONAL HOT SAUCE DAY
26 NATIONAL PEANUT BRITTLE DAY	**27** NATIONAL CHOCOLATE CAKE DAY	**28** NATIONAL KAZOO DAY	**29** CHINESE NEW YEAR: YEAR OF THE SNAKE NATIONAL PUZZLE DAY

Thursday	Friday	Saturday	NOTES
			○
			○
			○
2	**3**	**4**	○
			○
			○
Hanukkah ends at nightfall			
National Science Fiction Day	Happy Birthday to J.R.R. Tolkien!	National Trivia Day	
9	**10**	**11**	○
			○
			○
Law Enforcement Appreciation Day (L.E.A.D)	National Houseplant Appreciation Day	National Milk Day	
16	**17**	**18**	○
			○
			○
National Nothing Day	Popeye Day	Winne the Pooh Day	
23	**24**	**25**	○
			○
			○
National Handwriting Day	Global Belly Laugh Day	St. Dwynwen's Day	
30	**31**		○
			○
			○
National Croissant Day	National Backward Day		

December 2024 / January 2025   Week 1

Monday	December 30
Tuesday	December 31
Wednesday	January 1
Thursday	January 2
Friday	January 3
Saturday	January 4
Sunday	January 5

January 2025

Su	M	Tu	W	Th	F	Sa
			1	2	3	4
5	6	7	8	9	10	11
12	13	14	15	16	17	18
19	20	21	22	23	24	25
26	27	28	29	30	31	

January 2025

Monday | January 6

Tuesday | January 7

Wednesday | January 8

Thursday | January 9

Friday | January 10

Saturday | January 11

Sunday | January 12

January 2025

Su	M	Tu	W	Th	F	Sa
			1	2	3	4
5	6	7	8	9	10	11
12	13	14	15	16	17	18
19	20	21	22	23	24	25
26	27	28	29	30	31	

January 2025

Monday	January 13
Tuesday	January 14
Wednesday	January 15
Thursday	January 16
Friday	January 17
Saturday	January 18
Sunday	January 19

January 2025

Su	M	Tu	W	Th	F	Sa
			1	2	3	4
5	6	7	8	9	10	11
12	13	14	15	16	17	18
19	20	21	22	23	24	25
26	27	28	29	30	31	

January 2025

Week 4

Monday	January 20
Tuesday	January 21
Wednesday	January 22
Thursday	January 23
Friday	January 24
Saturday	January 25
Sunday	January 26

January 2025

Su	M	Tu	W	Th	F	Sa
			1	2	3	4
5	6	7	8	9	10	11
12	13	14	15	16	17	18
19	20	21	22	23	24	25
26	27	28	29	30	31	

January 2025

Week 5

Monday | January 27

Tuesday | January 28

Wednesday | January 29

Thursday | January 30

Friday | January 31

January 2025

Su	M	Tu	W	Th	F	Sa
			1	2	3	4
5	6	7	8	9	10	11
12	13	14	15	16	17	18
19	20	21	22	23	24	25
26	27	28	29	30	31	

February 2025

January 2025

Su	M	Tu	W	Th	F	Sa
			1	2	3	4
5	6	7	8	9	10	11
12	13	14	15	16	17	18
19	20	21	22	23	24	25
26	27	28	29	30	31	

March 2025

Su	M	Tu	W	Th	F	Sa
						1
2	3	4	5	6	7	8
9	10	11	12	13	14	15
16	17	18	19	20	21	22
23	24	25	26	27	28	29
30	31					

Sunday	Monday	Tuesday	Wednesday
IMPORTANT:			
2 Groundhog Day	**3** Happy Birthday to Elmo!	**4** Sweater Day	**5** World Nutella Day
9 National Pizza Day	**10** National Umbrella Day	**11** National Inventors' Day	**12** Lincoln's Birthday
16 National Almond Day	**17** National Random Acts Of Kindness Day Presidents' Day	**18** Pluto Day	**19** National Chocolate Mint Day
23 National Tootsie Roll Day	**24** National Tortilla Chip Day	**25** National Clam Chowder Day	**26** National Pistachio Day

IMPORTANT:

Thursday	Friday	Saturday
		1 NATIONAL FREEDOM DAY
6 NATIONAL CHOPSTICKS DAY	**7** NATIONAL FETTUCCINE ALFREDO DAY	**8** NATIONAL KITE-FLYING DAY
13 WORLD RADIO DAY	**14** VALENTINE'S DAY	**15** SUSAN B. ANTHONY DAY
20 NORTHERN HEMISPHERE HOODIE-HOO-DAY	**21** NATIONAL STICKY BUN DAY	**22** NATIONAL WALKING THE DOG DAY
27 NATIONAL RETRO DAY	**28** NATIONAL CHOCOLATE SOUFFLE DAY	

NOTES

Monday	January 27

Tuesday	January 28

Wednesday	January 29

Thursday	January 30

Friday	January 31

Saturday	**February 1**

Sunday	February 2

February 2025

Su	M	Tu	W	Th	F	Sa
						1
2	3	4	5	6	7	8
9	10	11	12	13	14	15
16	17	18	19	20	21	22
23	24	25	26	27	28	

February 2025

Monday	February 3
Tuesday	February 4
Wednesday	February 5
Thursday	February 6
Friday	February 7
Saturday	February 8
Sunday	February 9

February 2025

Su	M	Tu	W	Th	F	Sa
						1
2	3	4	5	6	7	8
9	10	11	12	13	14	15
16	17	18	19	20	21	22
23	24	25	26	27	28	

Monday	February 10

Tuesday	February 11

Wednesday	February 12

Thursday	February 13

Friday	February 14

Saturday	February 15

Sunday	February 16

February 2025

Su	M	Tu	W	Th	F	Sa
						1
2	3	4	5	6	7	8
9	10	11	12	13	14	15
16	17	18	19	20	21	22
23	24	25	26	27	28	

February 2025

Monday — February 17

Tuesday — February 18

Wednesday — February 19

Thursday — February 20

Friday — February 21

Saturday — February 22

Sunday — February 23

February 2025

Su	M	Tu	W	Th	F	Sa
						1
2	3	4	5	6	7	8
9	10	11	12	13	14	15
16	17	18	19	20	21	22
23	24	25	26	27	28	

Monday

February 24

Tuesday

February 25

Wednesday

February 26

Thursday

February 27

Friday

February 28

February 2025

Su	M	Tu	W	Th	F	Sa
						1
2	3	4	5	6	7	8
9	10	11	12	13	14	15
16	17	18	19	20	21	22
23	24	25	26	27	28	

March 2025

February 2025

Su	M	Tu	W	Th	F	Sa
						1
2	3	4	5	6	7	8
9	10	11	12	13	14	15
16	17	18	19	20	21	22
23	24	25	26	27	28	

April 2025

Su	M	Tu	W	Th	F	Sa
		1	2	3	4	5
6	7	8	9	10	11	12
13	14	15	16	17	18	19
20	21	22	23	24	25	26
27	28	29	30			

Sunday	Monday	Tuesday	Wednesday
IMPORTANT:			
2 NATIONAL BANANA CREAM PIE DAY	**3** WORLD WILDLIFE DAY	**4** NATIONAL GRAMMAR DAY	**5** NATIONAL CHEESE DOODLE DAY ASH WEDNESDAY
9 NATIONAL GET OVER IT DAY DAYLIGHT SAVING TIME BEGINS	**10** INTERNATIONAL BAGPIPE DAY	**11** NATIONAL DREAM DAY	**12** NATIONAL WORKING MOMS DAY
16 NATIONAL PANDA DAY	**17** ST. PATRICK'S DAY	**18** NATIONAL AWKWARD MOMENTS DAY	**19** NATIONAL LET'S LAUGH DAY
23 NATIONAL PUPPY DAY	**24** NATIONAL CHEESESTEAK DAY	**25** INTERNATIONAL WAFFLE DAY	**26** NATIONAL SPINACH DAY
30 TAKE A WALK IN THE PARK DAY	**31** NATIONAL TATER DAY		

Thursday	Friday	Saturday	NOTES
		1 NATIONAL PIG DAY	○ _____
6 NATIONAL OREO COOKIE DAY	**7** ALEXANDER GRAHAM BELL DAY	**8** NATIONAL PROOFREADING DAY	○ _____
13 NATIONAL GOOD SAMARITAN DAY PURIM BEGINS AT SUNSET	**14** NATIONAL PI DAY PURIM ENDS AT NIGHTFALL	**15** IDES OF MARCH	○ _____
20 WORLD FROG DAY SPRING BEGINS	**21** WORLD POETRY DAY	**22** NATIONAL GOOF OFF DAY	○ _____
27 NATIONAL SCRIBBLE DAY	**28** BARNUM & BAILEY DAY	**29** WORLD PIANO DAY	○ _____

IMPORTANT:

February /March 2025

Monday	February 24
Tuesday	February 25
Wednesday	February 26
Thursday	February 27
Friday	February 28
Saturday	March 1
Sunday	March 2

March 2025

Su	M	Tu	W	Th	F	Sa
						1
2	3	4	5	6	7	8
9	10	11	12	13	14	15
16	17	18	19	20	21	22
23	24	25	26	27	28	29
30	31					

Monday — March 3

Tuesday — March 4

Wednesday — March 5

Thursday — March 6

Friday — March 7

Saturday — March 8

Sunday — March 9

March 2025

Su	M	Tu	W	Th	F	Sa
						1
2	3	4	5	6	7	8
9	10	11	12	13	14	15
16	17	18	19	20	21	22
23	24	25	26	27	28	29
30	31					

Monday

March 10

Tuesday

March 11

Wednesday

March 12

Thursday

March 13

Friday

March 14

Saturday

March 15

Sunday

March 16

March 2025

Su	M	Tu	W	Th	F	Sa
						1
2	3	4	5	6	7	8
9	10	11	12	13	14	15
16	17	18	19	20	21	22
23	24	25	26	27	28	29
30	31					

March 2025

Monday	March 17
Tuesday	March 18
Wednesday	March 19
Thursday	March 20
Friday	March 21
Saturday	March 22
Sunday	March 23

March 2025

Su	M	Tu	W	Th	F	Sa
						1
2	3	4	5	6	7	8
9	10	11	12	13	14	15
16	17	18	19	20	21	22
23	24	25	26	27	28	29
30	31					

March 2025

Monday	March 24
Tuesday	March 25
Wednesday	March 26
Thursday	March 27
Friday	March 28
Saturday	March 29
Sunday	March 30

March 2025

Su	M	Tu	W	Th	F	Sa
						1
2	3	4	5	6	7	8
9	10	11	12	13	14	15
16	17	18	19	20	21	22
23	24	25	26	27	28	29
30	31					

Monday

March 31

Extra Notes for March

March 2025

Su	M	Tu	W	Th	F	Sa
						1
2	3	4	5	6	7	8
9	10	11	12	13	14	15
16	17	18	19	20	21	22
23	24	25	26	27	28	29
30	31					

April 2025

March 2025
Su	M	Tu	W	Th	F	Sa
						1
2	3	4	5	6	7	8
9	10	11	12	13	14	15
16	17	18	19	20	21	22
23	24	25	26	27	28	29
30	31					

May 2025
Su	M	Tu	W	Th	F	Sa
				1	2	3
4	5	6	7	8	9	10
11	12	13	14	15	16	17
18	19	20	21	22	23	24
25	26	27	28	29	30	31

Sunday	Monday	Tuesday	Wednesday
IMPORTANT:			
		1 April Fools' Day	**2** National Peanut Butter And Jelly Day
6 National Tartan Day	**7** International Beaver Day	**8** National Empanada Day	**9** National Unicorn Day
13 National Scrabble Day Palm Sunday	**14** National Look Up at the Sky Day	**15** National ASL Day	**16** Wear Pajamas to Work Day
20 National Look Alike Day Easter Sunday Passover Ends at Nightfall	**21** National Big Word Day	**22** Earth Day	**23** Shakespeare Day Administrative Professionals Day
27 Morse Code Day	**28** National Superhero Day	**29** International Dance Day	**30** International Jazz Day

Thursday	Friday	Saturday	NOTES
3 NATIONAL FILM SCORE DAY	**4** INTERNATIONAL CARROT DAY	**5** NATIONAL DEEP DISH PIZZA DAY	
10 SIBLINGS DAY	**11** NATIONAL PET DAY	**12** NATIONAL LICORICE DAY / PASSOVER BEGINS AT SUNSET	
17 INTERNATIONAL HAIKU POETRY DAY / MAUNDY THURSDAY	**18** NATIONAL ANIMAL CRACKER DAY / GOOD FRIDAY	**19** NATIONAL GARLIC DAY	
24 HAPPY BIRTHDAY TO BARBRA STREISAND!	**25** RED HAT SOCIETY DAY	**26** NATIONAL PRETZEL DAY	

IMPORTANT:

March / April 2025

Monday

March 31

Tuesday

April 1

Wednesday

April 2

Thursday

April 3

Friday

April 4

Saturday

April 5

Sunday

April 6

April 2025

Su	M	Tu	W	Th	F	Sa
		1	2	3	4	5
6	7	8	9	10	11	12
13	14	15	16	17	18	19
20	21	22	23	24	25	26
27	28	29	30			

Monday — April 7

Tuesday — April 8

Wednesday — April 9

Thursday — April 10

Friday — April 11

Saturday — April 12

Sunday — April 13

April 2025

Su	M	Tu	W	Th	F	Sa
		1	2	3	4	5
6	7	8	9	10	11	12
13	14	15	16	17	18	19
20	21	22	23	24	25	26
27	28	29	30			

April 2025

Monday
April 14

Tuesday
April 15

Wednesday
April 16

Thursday
April 17

Friday
April 18

Saturday
April 19

Sunday
April 20

April 2025

Su	M	Tu	W	Th	F	Sa
		1	2	3	4	5
6	7	8	9	10	11	12
13	14	15	16	17	18	19
20	21	22	23	24	25	26
27	28	29	30			

April 2025

Monday
April 21

Tuesday
April 22

Wednesday
April 23

Thursday
April 24

Friday
April 25

Saturday
April 26

Sunday
April 27

April 2025

Su	M	Tu	W	Th	F	Sa
		1	2	3	4	5
6	7	8	9	10	11	12
13	14	15	16	17	18	19
20	21	22	23	24	25	26
27	28	29	30			

Monday April 28

Tuesday April 29

Wednesday April 30

April 2025

Su	M	Tu	W	Th	F	Sa
		1	2	3	4	5
6	7	8	9	10	11	12
13	14	15	16	17	18	19
20	21	22	23	24	25	26
27	28	29	30			

May 2025

April 2025

Su	M	Tu	W	Th	F	Sa
		1	2	3	4	5
6	7	8	9	10	11	12
13	14	15	16	17	18	19
20	21	22	23	24	25	26
27	28	29	30			

June 2025

Su	M	Tu	W	Th	F	Sa
1	2	3	4	5	6	7
8	9	10	11	12	13	14
15	16	17	18	19	20	21
22	23	24	25	26	27	28
29	30					

Sunday	Monday	Tuesday	Wednesday
IMPORTANT:			
4 STAR WARS DAY	**5** CINCO DE MAYO	**6** INTERNATIONAL NO DIET DAY	**7** NATIONAL BARRIER AWARENESS DAY
11 TWILIGHT ZONE DAY MOTHER'S DAY	**12** NATIONAL LIMERICK DAY	**13** INTERNATIONAL HUMMUS DAY	**14** NATIONAL DANCE LIKE A CHICKEN DAY
18 I LOVE REESE'S DAY	**19** NATIONAL PLANT SOMETHING DAY	**20** WORLD BEE DAY	**21** NATIONAL TALK LIKE YODA DAY
25 TOWEL DAY	**26** NATIONAL PAPER AIRPLANE DAY MEMORIAL DAY	**27** NATIONAL CELLOPHANE TAPE DAY	**28** NATIONAL HAMBURGER DAY

Thursday	Friday	Saturday	NOTES
			○
			○
			○
1	**2**	**3**	○
			○
		NATIONAL TWO DIFFERENT COLORED SHOES DAY	○
MOTHER GOOSE DAY	INTERNATIONAL HARRY POTTER DAY	KENTUCKY DERBY	
8	**9**	**10**	○
			○
			○
NATIONAL IRIS DAY	NATIONAL SLEEPOVER DAY	NATIONAL CLEAN UP YOUR ROOM DAY	
15	**16**	**17**	○
			○
	NATIONAL DO SOMETHING GOOD FOR YOUR NEIGHBOR DAY	NATIONAL WALNUT DAY	○
NATIONAL CHOCOLATE CHIP DAY		ARMED FORCES DAY	
22	**23**	**24**	○
			○
			○
NATIONAL SOLITAIRE DAY	WORLD TURTLE DAY	NATIONAL ASPARAGUS DAY	
29	**30**	**31**	○
			○
NATIONAL ALLIGATOR DAY			○
ASCENSION DAY	NATIONAL CREATIVITY DAY	NATIONAL SMILE DAY	

April /May 2025

Monday — April 28

Tuesday — April 29

Wednesday — April 30

Thursday — May 1

Friday — May 2

Saturday — May 3

Sunday — May 4

May 2025

Su	M	Tu	W	Th	F	Sa
				1	2	3
4	5	6	7	8	9	10
11	12	13	14	15	16	17
18	19	20	21	22	23	24
25	26	27	28	29	30	31

Monday	May 5

Tuesday	May 6

Wednesday	May 7

Thursday	May 8

Friday	May 9

Saturday	May 10

Sunday	May 11

May 2025

Su	M	Tu	W	Th	F	Sa
				1	2	3
4	5	6	7	8	9	10
11	12	13	14	15	16	17
18	19	20	21	22	23	24
25	26	27	28	29	30	31

May 2025

Monday
May 12

Tuesday
May 13

Wednesday
May 14

Thursday
May 15

Friday
May 16

Saturday
May 17

Sunday
May 18

May 2025

Su	M	Tu	W	Th	F	Sa
				1	2	3
4	5	6	7	8	9	10
11	12	13	14	15	16	17
18	19	20	21	22	23	24
25	26	27	28	29	30	31

May 2025

Monday	May 19
Tuesday	May 20
Wednesday	May 21
Thursday	May 22
Friday	May 23
Saturday	May 24
Sunday	May 25

May 2025

Su	M	Tu	W	Th	F	Sa
				1	2	3
4	5	6	7	8	9	10
11	12	13	14	15	16	17
18	19	20	21	22	23	24
25	26	27	28	29	30	31

May 2025

Monday	May 26
Tuesday	May 27
Wednesday	May 28
Thursday	May 29
Friday	May 30
Saturday	May 31

May 2025

Su	M	Tu	W	Th	F	Sa
				1	2	3
4	5	6	7	8	9	10
11	12	13	14	15	16	17
18	19	20	21	22	23	24
25	26	27	28	29	30	31

June 2025

May 2024

Su	M	Tu	W	Th	F	Sa
				1	2	3
4	5	6	7	8	9	10
11	12	13	14	15	16	17
18	19	20	21	22	23	24
25	26	27	28	29	30	31

July 2025

Su	M	Tu	W	Th	F	Sa
		1	2	3	4	5
6	7	8	9	10	11	12
13	14	15	16	17	18	19
20	21	22	23	24	25	26
27	28	29	30	31		

Sunday	Monday	Tuesday	Wednesday
IMPORTANT:			
1 National Olive Day Shavuot Begins at Sunset	**2** National Rocky Road Day	**3** World Bicycle Day Shavuot Ends at Nightfall	**4** National Cheese Day
8 World Oceans Day Pentecost	**9** Happy Birthday to Donald Duck!	**10** National Iced Tea Day	**11** National Corn on the Cob Day
15 Father's Day Trinity Sunday	**16** National Fudge Day	**17** National Apple Strudel Day	**18** International Sushi Day
22 National Onion Ring Day	**23** Pink Flamingo Day	**24** International Fairy Day	**25** Global Beatles Day
29 National Camera Day	**30** International Asteroid Day		

> *My 4-year-old son gave me a handmade card for Father's Day.*
> *Maybe for Christmas I'll draw him a picture of some toys.* ~ Jim Gaffigan

Thursday	Friday	Saturday
5	**6**	**7**
National Gingerbread Day	National Yo-Yo Day	Daniel Boone Day
12	**13**	**14**
Superman Day	International Axe Throwing Day	Flag Day
19	**20** American Eagle Day	**21**
Juneteenth	Summer Begins	World Day of Music
26	**27**	**28**
National Coconut Day	National Bingo Day	Paul Bunyan Day

IMPORTANT:

NOTES

○
○
○
○
○
○
○
○
○
○
○
○
○
○
○
○
○

Monday	May 26
Tuesday	May 27
Wednesday	May 28
Thursday	May 29
Friday	May 30
Saturday	May 31
Sunday	June 1

June 2025

Su	M	Tu	W	Th	F	Sa
1	2	3	4	5	6	7
8	9	10	11	12	13	14
15	16	17	18	19	20	21
22	23	24	25	26	27	28
29	30					

Monday — June 2

Tuesday — June 3

Wednesday — June 4

Thursday — June 5

Friday — June 6

Saturday — June 7

Sunday — June 8

June 2025

Su	M	Tu	W	Th	F	Sa
1	2	3	4	5	6	7
8	9	10	11	12	13	14
15	16	17	18	19	20	21
22	23	24	25	26	27	28
29	30					

June 2025

Monday	June 9
Tuesday	June 10
Wednesday	June 11
Thursday	June 12
Friday	June 13
Saturday	June 14
Sunday	June 15

June 2025

Su	M	Tu	W	Th	F	Sa
1	2	3	4	5	6	7
8	9	10	11	12	13	14
15	16	17	18	19	20	21
22	23	24	25	26	27	28
29	30					

Monday
June 16

Tuesday
June 17

Wednesday
June 18

Thursday
June 19

Friday
June 20

Saturday
June 21

Sunday
June 22

June 2025

Su	M	Tu	W	Th	F	Sa
1	2	3	4	5	6	7
8	9	10	11	12	13	14
15	16	17	18	19	20	21
22	23	24	25	26	27	28
29	30					

Monday — June 23

Tuesday — June 24

Wednesday — June 25

Thursday — June 26

Friday — June 27

Saturday — June 28

Sunday — June 29

June 2025

Su	M	Tu	W	Th	F	Sa
1	2	3	4	5	6	7
8	9	10	11	12	13	14
15	16	17	18	19	20	21
22	23	24	25	26	27	28
29	30					

Monday

June 30

Extra Notes for June

June 2025

Su	M	Tu	W	Th	F	Sa
1	2	3	4	5	6	7
8	9	10	11	12	13	14
15	16	17	18	19	20	21
22	23	24	25	26	27	28
29	30					

July 2025

June 2025

Su	M	Tu	W	Th	F	Sa
1	2	3	4	5	6	7
8	9	10	11	12	13	14
15	16	17	18	19	20	21
22	23	24	25	26	27	28
29	30					

August 2025

Su	M	Tu	W	Th	F	Sa
					1	2
3	4	5	6	7	8	9
10	11	12	13	14	15	16
17	18	19	20	21	22	23
24	25	26	27	28	29	30
31						

Sunday	Monday	Tuesday	Wednesday
IMPORTANT:			
		1 INTERNATIONAL JOKE DAY	**2** WORLD UFO DAY
6 INTERNATIONAL KISSING DAY	**7** NATIONAL MACARONI DAY	**8** NATIONAL BLUEBERRY DAY	**9** NATIONAL SUGAR COOKIE DAY
13 NATIONAL BEANS 'N' FRANKS DAY	**14** BASTILLE DAY	**15** NATIONAL GIVE SOMETHING AWAY DAY	**16** GUINEA PIG APPRECIATION DAY
20 INTERNATIONAL MOON DAY	**21** NATIONAL JUNK FOOD DAY	**22** NATIONAL HAMMOCK DAY	**23** YADA YADA YADA DAY
27 BAGPIPE APPRECIATION DAY	**28** NATIONAL MILK CHOCOLATE DAY	**29** NATIONAL LASAGNA DAY	**30** NATIONAL CHEESECAKE DAY

Thursday	Friday	Saturday
3	**4**	**5**
NATIONAL STAY OUT OF THE SUN DAY	INDEPENDENCE DAY	NATIONAL GRAHAM CRACKER DAY
10	**11**	**12**
NATIONAL TEDDY BEAR PICNIC DAY	ALL AMERICAN PET PHOTO DAY	NATIONAL PECAN PIE DAY
17	**18**	**19**
WORLD EMOJI DAY	NATIONAL SOUR CANDY DAY	STICK OUT YOUR TONGUE DAY
24	**25**	**26**
COUSINS DAY	NATIONAL MERRY-GO-ROUND DAY	NATIONAL AUNT AND UNCLE DAY
31	IMPORTANT:	
NATIONAL AVOCADO DAY		

NOTES

June / July 2025

Monday | June 30

Tuesday | July 1

Wednesday | July 2

Thursday | July 3

Friday | July 4

Saturday | July 5

Sunday | July 6

July 2025

Su	M	Tu	W	Th	F	Sa
		1	2	3	4	5
6	7	8	9	10	11	12
13	14	15	16	17	18	19
20	21	22	23	24	25	26
27	28	29	30	31		

Monday

July 7

Tuesday

July 8

Wednesday

July 9

Thursday

July 10

Friday

July 11

Saturday

July 12

Sunday

July 13

July 2025

Su	M	Tu	W	Th	F	Sa
		1	2	3	4	5
6	7	8	9	10	11	12
13	14	15	16	17	18	19
20	21	22	23	24	25	26
27	28	29	30	31		

Monday
July 14

Tuesday
July 15

Wednesday
July 16

Thursday
July 17

Friday
July 18

Saturday
July 19

Sunday
July 20

July 2025

Su	M	Tu	W	Th	F	Sa
		1	2	3	4	5
6	7	8	9	10	11	12
13	14	15	16	17	18	19
20	21	22	23	24	25	26
27	28	29	30	31		

July 2025

Monday	July 21
Tuesday	July 22
Wednesday	July 23
Thursday	July 24
Friday	July 25
Saturday	July 26
Sunday	July 27

July 2025

Su	M	Tu	W	Th	F	Sa
		1	2	3	4	5
6	7	8	9	10	11	12
13	14	15	16	17	18	19
20	21	22	23	24	25	26
27	28	29	30	31		

Monday	July 28
Tuesday	July 29
Wednesday	July 30
Thursday	July 31

July 2025

Su	M	Tu	W	Th	F	Sa
		1	2	3	4	5
6	7	8	9	10	11	12
13	14	15	16	17	18	19
20	21	22	23	24	25	26
27	28	29	30	31		

August 2025

July 2025

Su	M	Tu	W	Th	F	Sa
		1	2	3	4	5
6	7	8	9	10	11	12
13	14	15	16	17	18	19
20	21	22	23	24	25	26
27	28	29	30	31		

September 2025

Su	M	Tu	W	Th	F	Sa
	1	2	3	4	5	6
7	8	9	10	11	12	13
14	15	16	17	18	19	20
21	22	23	24	25	26	27
28	29	30				

Sunday	Monday	Tuesday	Wednesday
IMPORTANT:			
3 NATIONAL WATERMELON DAY	**4** NATIONAL CHOCOLATE CHIP COOKIE DAY	**5** NATIONAL OYSTER DAY	**6** NATIONAL WIGGLE YOUR TOES DAY
10 NATIONAL S'MORES DAY	**11** HIP HOP CELEBRATION DAY	**12** WORLD ELEPHANT DAY	**13** LEFTHANDERS DAY
17 NATIONAL PINEAPPLE JUICE DAY	**18** NATIONAL FAJITA DAY	**19** NATIONAL POTATO DAY	**20** WORLD MOSQUITO DAY
24 WILLIAM WILBERFORCE DAY	**25** NATIONAL BANANA SPLIT DAY	**26** NATIONAL TOILET PAPER DAY	**27** NATIONAL JUST BECAUSE DAY
31 NATIONAL EAT OUTSIDE DAY	**IMPORTANT:**		

Thursday	Friday	Saturday
	1	2
	SPIDER-MAN DAY	NATIONAL COLORING BOOK DAY
7	8	9
NATIONAL LIGHTHOUSE DAY	INTERNATIONAL CAT DAY	NATIONAL BOOK LOVERS DAY
14	15	16
NATIONAL NAVAJO CODE TALKERS DAY	NATIONAL RELAXATION DAY	NATIONAL TELL A JOKE DAY
21	22	23
NATIONAL SENIOR CITIZENS DAY	NATIONAL BAO DAY	FIND YOUR INNER NERD DAY
28	29	30
NATIONAL BOW TIE DAY	NATIONAL LEMON JUICE DAY	SLINKY DAY

NOTES

Monday	July 28
Tuesday	July 29
Wednesday	July 30
Thursday	July 31
Friday	August 1
Saturday	August 2
Sunday	August 3

August 2025

Su	M	Tu	W	Th	F	Sa
					1	2
3	4	5	6	7	8	9
10	11	12	13	14	15	16
17	18	19	20	21	22	23
24	25	26	27	28	29	30
31						

Monday	August 4
Tuesday	August 5
Wednesday	August 6
Thursday	August 7
Friday	August 8
Saturday	August 9
Sunday	August 10

August 2025

Su	M	Tu	W	Th	F	Sa
					1	2
3	4	5	6	7	8	9
10	11	12	13	14	15	16
17	18	19	20	21	22	23
24	25	26	27	28	29	30
31						

Monday — August 11

Tuesday — August 12

Wednesday — August 13

Thursday — August 14

Friday — August 15

Saturday — August 16

Sunday — August 17

August 2025

Su	M	Tu	W	Th	F	Sa
					1	2
3	4	5	6	7	8	9
10	11	12	13	14	15	16
17	18	19	20	21	22	23
24	25	26	27	28	29	30
31						

Monday — August 18

Tuesday — August 19

Wednesday — August 20

Thursday — August 21

Friday — August 22

Saturday — August 23

Sunday — August 24

August 2025

Su	M	Tu	W	Th	F	Sa
					1	2
3	4	5	6	7	8	9
10	11	12	13	14	15	16
17	18	19	20	21	22	23
24	25	26	27	28	29	30
31						

Monday | August 25

Tuesday | August 26

Wednesday | August 27

Thursday | August 28

Friday | August 29

Saturday | August 30

Sunday | August 31

August 2025

Su	M	Tu	W	Th	F	Sa
					1	2
3	4	5	6	7	8	9
10	11	12	13	14	15	16
17	18	19	20	21	22	23
24	25	26	27	28	29	30
31						

September 2025

August 2025

Su	M	Tu	W	Th	F	Sa
					1	2
3	4	5	6	7	8	9
10	11	12	13	14	15	16
17	18	19	20	21	22	23
24	25	26	27	28	29	30
31						

October 2025

Su	M	Tu	W	Th	F	Sa
			1	2	3	4
5	6	7	8	9	10	11
12	13	14	15	16	17	18
19	20	21	22	23	24	25
26	27	28	29	30	31	

Sunday	Monday	Tuesday	Wednesday
IMPORTANT:			
	1 AMERICAN CHESS DAY LABOR DAY	**2** WORLD COCONUT DAY	**3** NATIONAL SKYSCRAPER DAY
7 NATIONAL SALAMI DAY	**8** INTERNATIONAL LITERACY DAY	**9** NATIONAL TEDDY BEAR DAY	**10** NATIONAL TV DINNER DAY
14 NATIONAL CREAM-FILLED DONUT DAY	**15** GREENPEACE DAY	**16** NATIONAL PLAY-DOH DAY	**17** NATIONAL APPLE DUMPLING DAY
21 NATIONAL CHAI DAY	**22** HOBBIT DAY AUTUMN BEGINS ROSH HASHANAH BEGINS AT SUNSET	**23** INTERNATIONAL DAY OF SIGN LANGUAGES	**24** NATIONAL PUNCTUATION DAY ROSH HASHANAH ENDS AT NIGHTFALL
28 NATIONAL GOOD NEIGHBOR DAY	**29** NATIONAL BISCOTTI DAY	**30** NATIONAL CHEWING GUM DAY	

Thursday	Friday	Saturday
4	5	6
NATIONAL MACADAMIA NUT DAY	INTERNATIONAL DAY OF CHARITY	NATIONAL READ A BOOK DAY
11	12	13
PATRIOT DAY	NATIONAL VIDEO GAMES DAY	ROALD DAHL DAY
18	19	20
NATIONAL CHEESEBURGER DAY	NATIONAL TALK LIKE A PIRATE DAY	NATIONAL PEPPERONI PIZZA DAY
25	26	27
NATIONAL ONE HIT WONDER DAY	LUMBERJACK DAY	NATIONAL SCARF DAY

IMPORTANT:

NOTES

September 2025

Monday	September 1
Tuesday	September 2
Wednesday	September 3
Thursday	September 4
Friday	September 5
Saturday	September 6
Sunday	September 7

September 2025

Su	M	Tu	W	Th	F	Sa
	1	2	3	4	5	6
7	8	9	10	11	12	13
14	15	16	17	18	19	20
21	22	23	24	25	26	27
28	29	30				

Monday	September 8

Tuesday	September 9

Wednesday	September 10

Thursday	September 11

Friday	September 12

Saturday	September 13

Sunday	September 14

September 2025

Su	M	Tu	W	Th	F	Sa
	1	2	3	4	5	6
7	8	9	10	11	12	13
14	15	16	17	18	19	20
21	22	23	24	25	26	27
28	29	30				

Monday

September 15

Tuesday

September 16

Wednesday

September 17

Thursday

September 18

Friday

September 19

Saturday

September 20

Sunday

September 21

September 2025

Su	M	Tu	W	Th	F	Sa
	1	2	3	4	5	6
7	8	9	10	11	12	13
14	15	16	17	18	19	20
21	22	23	24	25	26	27
28	29	30				

Monday	September 22
Tuesday	September 23
Wednesday	September 24
Thursday	September 25
Friday	September 26
Saturday	September 27
Sunday	September 28

September 2025

Su	M	Tu	W	Th	F	Sa
	1	2	3	4	5	6
7	8	9	10	11	12	13
14	15	16	17	18	19	20
21	22	23	24	25	26	27
28	29	30				

Monday

September 29

Tuesday

September 30

September 2025

Su	M	Tu	W	Th	F	Sa
	1	2	3	4	5	6
7	8	9	10	11	12	13
14	15	16	17	18	19	20
21	22	23	24	25	26	27
28	29	30				

October 2025

September 2025

Su	M	Tu	W	Th	F	Sa
	1	2	3	4	5	6
7	8	9	10	11	12	13
14	15	16	17	18	19	20
21	22	23	24	25	26	27
28	29	30				

November 2025

Su	M	Tu	W	Th	F	Sa
						1
2	3	4	5	6	7	8
9	10	11	12	13	14	15
16	17	18	19	20	21	22
23	24	25	26	27	28	29
30						

Sunday	Monday	Tuesday	Wednesday
IMPORTANT:			
			1 INTERNATIONAL COFFEE DAY YOM KIPPUR BEGINS AT SUNSET
5 NATIONAL GET FUNKY DAY	**6** NATIONAL NOODLE DAY SUKKOT BEGINS AT SUNSET	**7** WORLD COTTON DAY	**8** NATIONAL FLUFFERNUTTER DAY
12 NATIONAL FARMER'S DAY	**13** NATIONAL TRAIN YOUR BRAIN DAY COLUMBUS DAY SUKKOT ENDS AT NIGHTFALL	**14** NATIONAL DESSERT DAY	**15** I LOVE LUCY DAY
19 NATIONAL NEW FRIENDS DAY	**20** NATIONAL DAY ON WRITING	**21** BACK TO THE FUTURE DAY	**22** NATIONAL NUT DAY
26 NATIONAL PUMPKIN DAY	**27** NATIONAL BLACK CAT DAY	**28** INTERNATIONAL ANIMATION DAY	**29** NATIONAL OATMEAL DAY

Thursday	Friday	Saturday	NOTES
			○
			○
			○
2	**3**	**4**	○
			○
NATIONAL NAME YOUR CAR DAY			○
YOM KIPPUR ENDS AT NIGHTFALL	NATIONAL BOYFRIEND DAY	NATIONAL CINNAMON ROLL DAY	
9	**10**	**11**	○
			○
			○
NATIONAL MOLDY CHEESE DAY	NATIONAL CAKE DECORATING DAY	SOUTHERN FOOD HERITAGE DAY	
16	**17**	**18**	○
			○
	NATIONAL WEAR SOMETHING GAUDY DAY		○
DICTIONARY DAY		NATIONAL CHOCOLATE CUPCAKE DAY	
23	**24**	**25**	○
			○
			○
NATIONAL BOSTON CREAM PIE DAY	NATIONAL BOLOGNA DAY	WORLD OPERA DAY	
30	**31**		○
			○
NATIONAL CANDY CORN DAY	HALLOWEEN		○

September / October 2025

Week 1

Monday	September 29
Tuesday	September 30
Wednesday	October 1
Thursday	October 2
Friday	October 3
Saturday	October 4
Sunday	October 5

October 2025

Su	M	Tu	W	Th	F	Sa
			1	2	3	4
5	6	7	8	9	10	11
12	13	14	15	16	17	18
19	20	21	22	23	24	25
26	27	28	29	30	31	

Monday	October 6
Tuesday	October 7
Wednesday	October 8
Thursday	October 9
Friday	October 10
Saturday	October 11
Sunday	October 12

October 2025

Su	M	Tu	W	Th	F	Sa
			1	2	3	4
5	6	7	8	9	10	11
12	13	14	15	16	17	18
19	20	21	22	23	24	25
26	27	28	29	30	31	

Monday	October 13
Tuesday	October 14
Wednesday	October 15
Thursday	October 16
Friday	October 17
Saturday	October 18
Sunday	October 19

October 2025

Su	M	Tu	W	Th	F	Sa
			1	2	3	4
5	6	7	8	9	10	11
12	13	14	15	16	17	18
19	20	21	22	23	24	25
26	27	28	29	30	31	

October 2025

Monday	October 20
Tuesday	October 21
Wednesday	October 22
Thursday	October 23
Friday	October 24
Saturday	October 25
Sunday	October 26

October 2025

Su	M	Tu	W	Th	F	Sa
			1	2	3	4
5	6	7	8	9	10	11
12	13	14	15	16	17	18
19	20	21	22	23	24	25
26	27	28	29	30	31	

Monday — October 27

Tuesday — October 28

Wednesday — October 29

Thursday — October 30

Friday — October 31

October 2025

Su	M	Tu	W	Th	F	Sa
			1	2	3	4
5	6	7	8	9	10	11
12	13	14	15	16	17	18
19	20	21	22	23	24	25
26	27	28	29	30	31	

November 2025

October 2025
Su	M	Tu	W	Th	F	Sa
			1	2	3	4
5	6	7	8	9	10	11
12	13	14	15	16	17	18
19	20	21	22	23	24	25
26	27	28	29	30	31	

December 2025
Su	M	Tu	W	Th	F	Sa
	1	2	3	4	5	6
7	8	9	10	11	12	13
14	15	16	17	18	19	20
21	22	23	24	25	26	27
28	29	30	31			

Sunday	Monday	Tuesday	Wednesday
IMPORTANT:			
2 NATIONAL DEVILED EGG DAY DAYLIGHT SAVINGS TIME ENDS (unless the Sunshine Protection Act passes)	**3** NATIONAL SANDWICH DAY	**4** NATIONAL CANDY DAY	**5** NATIONAL CHINESE TAKE-OUT DAY
9 NATIONAL SCRAPPLE DAY	**10** SESAME STREET DAY	**11** NATIONAL ORIGAMI DAY VETERANS DAY	**12** NATIONAL FRENCH DIP DAY
16 NATIONAL BUTTON DAY	**17** NATIONAL TAKE A HIKE DAY	**18** HAPPY BIRTHDAY TO MICKEY MOUSE!	**19** WORLD TOILET DAY
23 FIBONACCI DAY	**24** CELEBRATE YOUR UNIQUE TALENT DAY	**25** NATIONAL PARFAIT DAY	**26** NATIONAL CAKE DAY
30 NATIONAL MASON JAR DAY ADVENT	**IMPORTANT:**		

Thursday	Friday	Saturday	NOTES
		1 NATIONAL CINNAMON DAY ALL SAINTS' DAY	O O O
6 NATIONAL SAXOPHONE DAY	**7** NATIONAL HUG A BEAR DAY	**8** NATIONAL CAPPUCCINO DAY	O O O
13 WORLD KINDNESS DAY	**14** NATIONAL PICKLE DAY	**15** AMERICA RECYCLES DAY	O O O
20 NATIONAL PEANUT BUTTER FUDGE DAY	**21** WORLD TELEVISION DAY	**22** NATIONAL GO FOR A RIDE DAY	O O O
27 NATIONAL BAVARIAN CREAM PIE DAY THANKSGIVING DAY	**28** NATIONAL RED PLANET DAY	**29** SQUARE DANCING DAY	O O O
			O O O

October /November 2025   Week 1

Monday	October 27
Tuesday	October 28
Wednesday	October 29
Thursday	October 30
Friday	October 31
Saturday	November 1
Sunday	November 2

November 2025

Su	M	Tu	W	Th	F	Sa
						1
2	3	4	5	6	7	8
9	10	11	12	13	14	15
16	17	18	19	20	21	22
23	24	25	26	27	28	29
30						

Monday | November 3

Tuesday | November 4

Wednesday | November 5

Thursday | November 6

Friday | November 7

Saturday | November 8

Sunday | November 9

November 2025

Su	M	Tu	W	Th	F	Sa
						1
2	3	4	5	6	7	8
9	10	11	12	13	14	15
16	17	18	19	20	21	22
23	24	25	26	27	28	29
30						

Monday

November 10

Tuesday

November 11

Wednesday

November 12

Thursday

November 13

Friday

November 14

Saturday

November 15

Sunday

November 16

November 2025

Su	M	Tu	W	Th	F	Sa
						1
2	3	4	5	6	7	8
9	10	11	12	13	14	15
16	17	18	19	20	21	22
23	24	25	26	27	28	29
30						

Monday — November 17

Tuesday — November 18

Wednesday — November 19

Thursday — November 20

Friday — November 21

Saturday — November 22

Sunday — November 23

November 2025

Su	M	Tu	W	Th	F	Sa
						1
2	3	4	5	6	7	8
9	10	11	12	13	14	15
16	17	18	19	20	21	22
23	24	25	26	27	28	29
30						

Monday — November 24

Tuesday — November 25

Wednesday — November 26

Thursday — November 27

Friday — November 28

Saturday — November 29

Sunday — November 30

November 2025

Su	M	Tu	W	Th	F	Sa
						1
2	3	4	5	6	7	8
9	10	11	12	13	14	15
16	17	18	19	20	21	22
23	24	25	26	27	28	29
30						

December 2025

November 2025

Su	M	Tu	W	Th	F	Sa
						1
2	3	4	5	6	7	8
9	10	11	12	13	14	15
16	17	18	19	20	21	22
23	24	25	26	27	28	29
30						

January 2026

Su	M	Tu	W	Th	F	Sa
				1	2	3
4	5	6	7	8	9	10
11	12	13	14	15	16	17
18	19	20	21	22	23	24
25	26	27	28	29	30	31

Sunday	Monday	Tuesday	Wednesday
IMPORTANT:			
	1 Rosa Parks Day	**2** National Fritters Day	**3** Anniversary of First Text Message (1992)
7 Pearl Harbor Remembrance Day	**8** National Brownie Day	**9** National Llama Day	**10** Dewey Decimal System Day
14 Monkey Day Hanukkah begins at sunset	**15** National Cupcake Day	**16** National Chocolate-Covered Anything Day	**17** National Maple Syrup Day
21 NATIONAL FLASHLIGHT DAY Winter Begins	**22** National Cookie Exchange Day Hanukkah ends at nightfall	**23** Festivus	**24** Christmas Eve
28 National Call a Friend Day	**29** International Cello Day	**30** National Bacon Day	**31** New Year's Eve

Thursday	Friday	Saturday
4	**5**	**6**
NATIONAL COOKIE DAY	HAPPY BIRTHDAY TO WALT DISNEY!	SAINT NICHOLAS DAY
11	**12**	**13**
INTERNATIONAL MOUNTAIN DAY	NATIONAL DING-A-LING DAY	NATIONAL VIOLIN DAY
18	**19**	**20**
ANSWER THE TELEPHONE LIKE BUDDY THE ELF DAY	NATIONAL OATMEAL MUFFIN DAY	GO CAROLING DAY
25	**26**	**27**
	BOXING DAY	
CHRISTMAS DAY	KWANZAA BEGINS	NATIONAL FRUITCAKE DAY

IMPORTANT:

NOTES

○
○
○
○
○
○
○
○
○
○
○
○
○
○
○
○
○
○

December 2025

Week 1

Monday	December 1
Tuesday	December 2
Wednesday	December 3
Thursday	December 4
Friday	December 5
Saturday	December 6
Sunday	December 7

December 2025

Su	M	Tu	W	Th	F	Sa
	1	2	3	4	5	6
7	8	9	10	11	12	13
14	15	16	17	18	19	20
21	22	23	24	25	26	27
28	29	30	31			

Monday

December 8

Tuesday

December 9

Wednesday

December 10

Thursday

December 11

Friday

December 12

Saturday

December 13

Sunday

December 14

December 2025

Su	M	Tu	W	Th	F	Sa
	1	2	3	4	5	6
7	8	9	10	11	12	13
14	15	16	17	18	19	20
21	22	23	24	25	26	27
28	29	30	31			

Monday

December 15

Tuesday

December 16

Wednesday

December 17

Thursday

December 18

Friday

December 19

Saturday

December 20

Sunday

December 21

December 2025

Su	M	Tu	W	Th	F	Sa
	1	2	3	4	5	6
7	8	9	10	11	12	13
14	15	16	17	18	19	20
21	22	23	24	25	26	27
28	29	30	31			

Monday	December 22
Tuesday	December 23
Wednesday	December 24
Thursday	December 25
Friday	December 26
Saturday	December 27
Sunday	December 28

December 2025

Su	M	Tu	W	Th	F	Sa
	1	2	3	4	5	6
7	8	9	10	11	12	13
14	15	16	17	18	19	20
21	22	23	24	25	26	27
28	29	30	31			

December 2025

Monday
December 29

Tuesday
December 30

Wednesday
December 31

December 2025

Su	M	Tu	W	Th	F	Sa
	1	2	3	4	5	6
7	8	9	10	11	12	13
14	15	16	17	18	19	20
21	22	23	24	25	26	27
28	29	30	31			

Important People, Places, and Things

Important People, Places, and Things

Important People, Places, and Things

Important People, Places, and Things

Important People, Places, and Things

Bullet It!

Bullet It!

Bullet It!

Bullet It!

EVERY DAY IS A PARTY 2025 Appointment Calendar with Daily Party-Worthy Holidays: 8x10 Weekly Planner Featuring Fun Celebrations Like Squirrel Appreciation Day!

Graphics:
Front cover image: #3426459 by pineapplesupplyco from Pixabay.
Back cover image: #629946 by SevenStorm JUHASZIMRUS from Pexels.
            #6042301 by PandannaImagen from Pixabay.

ISBN: 978-1-947566-41-5
Published by Fermata House: Versailles, Kentucky

Fermata House
fermatahouse.com

Your suggestions and feedback are invaluable!

Any suggestions for next year's calendar themes?
Any important dates that we need to include in next year's calendar?

Please reach out through the contact form at fermatahouse.com.

Enjoy!

And please take the time to <u>leave a review</u> on Amazon.

Thanks!

See you next year!

Made in United States
Troutdale, OR
01/08/2025

27695240R00067